LIBRARY LENDING JOURNAL

FOR BOOKS, DVDs, TOOLS, ETC..

this book belongs to

address

phone

office

cell

designed by Clara Brayton

December 2025

ISBN 978-1-966639-00-5

BORROWER AND INFO	ITEM LOANED

NOTES	CONDITION OF ITEM
DATE OUT DATE BACK	P G F E OUT BACK LOAN TO AGAIN Y N

BORROWER AND INFO	ITEM LOANED

NOTES	CONDITION OF ITEM
DATE OUT DATE BACK	P G F E OUT BACK LOAN TO AGAIN Y N

KEY FOR CONDITION OF ITEM P=POOR G=GOOD F=FAIR E=EXCELLENT

BORROWER AND INFO	ITEM LOANED

NOTES	CONDITION OF ITEM
DATE OUT DATE BACK	P G F E OUT ☐ ☐ ☐ ☐ BACK ☐ ☐ ☐ ☐ LOAN TO AGAIN Y ☐ N ☐

BORROWER AND INFO	ITEM LOANED

NOTES	CONDITION OF ITEM
DATE OUT DATE BACK	P G F E OUT ☐ ☐ ☐ ☐ BACK ☐ ☐ ☐ ☐ LOAN TO AGAIN Y ☐ N ☐

KEY FOR CONDITION OF ITEM P=POOR G=GOOD F=FAIR E=EXCELLENT

BORROWER AND INFO	ITEM LOANED

NOTES	CONDITION OF ITEM
DATE OUT DATE BACK	

	P	G	F	E
OUT				
BACK				

LOAN TO AGAIN	Y		N	

BORROWER AND INFO	ITEM LOANED

NOTES	CONDITION OF ITEM
DATE OUT DATE BACK	

	P	G	F	E
OUT				
BACK				

LOAN TO AGAIN	Y		N	

KEY FOR CONDITION OF ITEM P=POOR G=GOOD F=FAIR E=EXCELLENT

BORROWER AND INFO	ITEM LOANED

NOTES	CONDITION OF ITEM
DATE OUT DATE BACK	P G F E OUT ☐☐☐☐ BACK ☐☐☐☐ LOAN TO AGAIN Y ☐ N ☐

BORROWER AND INFO	ITEM LOANED

NOTES	CONDITION OF ITEM
DATE OUT DATE BACK	P G F E OUT ☐☐☐☐ BACK ☐☐☐☐ LOAN TO AGAIN Y ☐ N ☐

KEY FOR CONDITION OF ITEM P=POOR G=GOOD F=FAIR E=EXCELLENT

BORROWER AND INFO	ITEM LOANED

NOTES	CONDITION OF ITEM
DATE OUT DATE BACK	P G F E OUT BACK LOAN TO AGAIN Y N

BORROWER AND INFO	ITEM LOANED

NOTES	CONDITION OF ITEM
DATE OUT DATE BACK	P G F E OUT BACK LOAN TO AGAIN Y N

KEY FOR CONDITION OF ITEM P=POOR G=GOOD F=FAIR E=EXCELLENT

BORROWER AND INFO	ITEM LOANED

NOTES	CONDITION OF ITEM
DATE OUT DATE BACK	P G F E OUT ☐☐☐☐ BACK ☐☐☐☐ LOAN TO AGAIN Y ☐ N ☐

BORROWER AND INFO	ITEM LOANED

NOTES	CONDITION OF ITEM
DATE OUT DATE BACK	P G F E OUT ☐☐☐☐ BACK ☐☐☐☐ LOAN TO AGAIN Y ☐ N ☐

KEY FOR CONDITION OF ITEM P=POOR G=GOOD F=FAIR E=EXCELLENT

BORROWER AND INFO	ITEM LOANED

NOTES	CONDITION OF ITEM
DATE OUT DATE BACK	P G F E OUT ☐ ☐ ☐ ☐ BACK ☐ ☐ ☐ ☐ LOAN TO AGAIN Y ☐ N ☐

BORROWER AND INFO	ITEM LOANED

NOTES	CONDITION OF ITEM
DATE OUT DATE BACK	P G F E OUT ☐ ☐ ☐ ☐ BACK ☐ ☐ ☐ ☐ LOAN TO AGAIN Y ☐ N ☐

KEY FOR CONDITION OF ITEM P=POOR G=GOOD F=FAIR E=EXCELLENT

BORROWER AND INFO	ITEM LOANED

NOTES	CONDITION OF ITEM
DATE OUT DATE BACK	P G F E OUT ☐☐☐☐ BACK ☐☐☐☐ LOAN TO AGAIN Y ☐ N ☐

BORROWER AND INFO	ITEM LOANED

NOTES	CONDITION OF ITEM
DATE OUT DATE BACK	P G F E OUT ☐☐☐☐ BACK ☐☐☐☐ LOAN TO AGAIN Y ☐ N ☐

KEY FOR CONDITION OF ITEM P=POOR G=GOOD F=FAIR E=EXCELLENT

BORROWER AND INFO

ITEM LOANED

NOTES

DATE OUT

DATE BACK

CONDITION OF ITEM

	P	G	F	E
OUT				
BACK				

LOAN TO AGAIN Y N

BORROWER AND INFO

ITEM LOANED

NOTES

DATE OUT

DATE BACK

CONDITION OF ITEM

	P	G	F	E
OUT				
BACK				

LOAN TO AGAIN Y N

KEY FOR CONDITION OF ITEM P=POOR G=GOOD F=FAIR E=EXCELLENT

BORROWER AND INFO	ITEM LOANED

NOTES	CONDITION OF ITEM
DATE OUT DATE BACK	P G F E OUT ☐☐☐☐ BACK ☐☐☐☐ LOAN TO AGAIN Y ☐ N ☐

BORROWER AND INFO	ITEM LOANED

NOTES	CONDITION OF ITEM
DATE OUT DATE BACK	P G F E OUT ☐☐☐☐ BACK ☐☐☐☐ LOAN TO AGAIN Y ☐ N ☐

KEY FOR CONDITION OF ITEM P=POOR G=GOOD F=FAIR E=EXCELLENT

BORROWER AND INFO	ITEM LOANED

NOTES	CONDITION OF ITEM
DATE OUT DATE BACK	

	P	G	F	E
OUT				
BACK				
LOAN TO AGAIN	Y		N	

BORROWER AND INFO	ITEM LOANED

NOTES	CONDITION OF ITEM
DATE OUT DATE BACK	

	P	G	F	E
OUT				
BACK				
LOAN TO AGAIN	Y		N	

KEY FOR CONDITION OF ITEM P=POOR G=GOOD F=FAIR E=EXCELLENT

BORROWER AND INFO	ITEM LOANED

NOTES	CONDITION OF ITEM
DATE OUT DATE BACK	P G F E OUT ☐☐☐☐ BACK ☐☐☐☐ LOAN TO AGAIN Y ☐ N ☐

BORROWER AND INFO	ITEM LOANED

NOTES	CONDITION OF ITEM
DATE OUT DATE BACK	P G F E OUT ☐☐☐☐ BACK ☐☐☐☐ LOAN TO AGAIN Y ☐ N ☐

KEY FOR CONDITION OF ITEM P=POOR G=GOOD F=FAIR E=EXCELLENT

BORROWER AND INFO | ITEM LOANED

NOTES

DATE OUT

DATE BACK

CONDITION OF ITEM

	P	G	F	E
OUT				
BACK				

LOAN TO AGAIN Y N

BORROWER AND INFO | ITEM LOANED

NOTES

DATE OUT

DATE BACK

CONDITION OF ITEM

	P	G	F	E
OUT				
BACK				

LOAN TO AGAIN Y N

KEY FOR CONDITION OF ITEM P=POOR G=GOOD F=FAIR E=EXCELLENT

BORROWER AND INFO	ITEM LOANED

NOTES	CONDITION OF ITEM
DATE OUT DATE BACK	

	P	G	F	E
OUT				
BACK				
LOAN TO AGAIN	Y		N	

BORROWER AND INFO	ITEM LOANED

NOTES	CONDITION OF ITEM
DATE OUT DATE BACK	

	P	G	F	E
OUT				
BACK				
LOAN TO AGAIN	Y		N	

KEY FOR CONDITION OF ITEM P=POOR G=GOOD F=FAIR E=EXCELLENT

BORROWER AND INFO	ITEM LOANED

NOTES	CONDITION OF ITEM
DATE OUT DATE BACK	P G F E OUT BACK LOAN TO AGAIN Y N

BORROWER AND INFO	ITEM LOANED

NOTES	CONDITION OF ITEM
DATE OUT DATE BACK	P G F E OUT BACK LOAN TO AGAIN Y N

KEY FOR CONDITION OF ITEM P=POOR G=GOOD F=FAIR E=EXCELLENT

BORROWER AND INFO	ITEM LOANED

NOTES	CONDITION OF ITEM
DATE OUT DATE BACK	P G F E OUT ☐ ☐ ☐ ☐ BACK ☐ ☐ ☐ ☐ LOAN TO AGAIN Y ☐ N ☐

BORROWER AND INFO	ITEM LOANED

NOTES	CONDITION OF ITEM
DATE OUT DATE BACK	P G F E OUT ☐ ☐ ☐ ☐ BACK ☐ ☐ ☐ ☐ LOAN TO AGAIN Y ☐ N ☐

KEY FOR CONDITION OF ITEM P=POOR G=GOOD F=FAIR E=EXCELLENT

BORROWER AND INFO	ITEM LOANED

NOTES	CONDITION OF ITEM
DATE OUT DATE BACK	

	P	G	F	E
OUT				
BACK				
LOAN TO AGAIN	Y		N	

BORROWER AND INFO	ITEM LOANED

NOTES	CONDITION OF ITEM
DATE OUT DATE BACK	

	P	G	F	E
OUT				
BACK				
LOAN TO AGAIN	Y		N	

KEY FOR CONDITION OF ITEM P=POOR G=GOOD F=FAIR E=EXCELLENT

BORROWER AND INFO	ITEM LOANED

NOTES	CONDITION OF ITEM
DATE OUT DATE BACK	P G F E OUT ☐☐☐☐ BACK ☐☐☐☐ LOAN TO AGAIN Y ☐ N ☐

BORROWER AND INFO	ITEM LOANED

NOTES	CONDITION OF ITEM
DATE OUT DATE BACK	P G F E OUT ☐☐☐☐ BACK ☐☐☐☐ LOAN TO AGAIN Y ☐ N ☐

KEY FOR CONDITION OF ITEM P=POOR G=GOOD F=FAIR E=EXCELLENT

BORROWER AND INFO	ITEM LOANED

NOTES	CONDITION OF ITEM
DATE OUT DATE BACK	P G F E OUT ☐ ☐ ☐ ☐ BACK ☐ ☐ ☐ ☐ LOAN TO AGAIN Y ☐ N ☐

BORROWER AND INFO	ITEM LOANED

NOTES	CONDITION OF ITEM
DATE OUT DATE BACK	P G F E OUT ☐ ☐ ☐ ☐ BACK ☐ ☐ ☐ ☐ LOAN TO AGAIN Y ☐ N ☐

KEY FOR CONDITION OF ITEM P=POOR G=GOOD F=FAIR E=EXCELLENT

BORROWER AND INFO

ITEM LOANED

NOTES

DATE OUT

DATE BACK

CONDITION OF ITEM

	P	G	F	E
OUT				
BACK				

LOAN TO AGAIN Y N

BORROWER AND INFO

ITEM LOANED

NOTES

DATE OUT

DATE BACK

CONDITION OF ITEM

	P	G	F	E
OUT				
BACK				

LOAN TO AGAIN Y N

KEY FOR CONDITION OF ITEM P=POOR G=GOOD F=FAIR E=EXCELLENT

BORROWER AND INFO	ITEM LOANED

NOTES	CONDITION OF ITEM
DATE OUT DATE BACK	P G F E OUT ☐☐☐☐ BACK ☐☐☐☐ LOAN TO AGAIN Y ☐ N ☐

BORROWER AND INFO	ITEM LOANED

NOTES	CONDITION OF ITEM
DATE OUT DATE BACK	P G F E OUT ☐☐☐☐ BACK ☐☐☐☐ LOAN TO AGAIN Y ☐ N ☐

KEY FOR CONDITION OF ITEM P=POOR G=GOOD F=FAIR E=EXCELLENT

BORROWER AND INFO	ITEM LOANED

NOTES	CONDITION OF ITEM
DATE OUT DATE BACK	

	P	G	F	E
OUT				
BACK				
LOAN TO AGAIN	Y		N	

BORROWER AND INFO	ITEM LOANED

NOTES	CONDITION OF ITEM
DATE OUT DATE BACK	

	P	G	F	E
OUT				
BACK				
LOAN TO AGAIN	Y		N	

KEY FOR CONDITION OF ITEM P=POOR G=GOOD F=FAIR E=EXCELLENT

BORROWER AND INFO

ITEM LOANED

NOTES

DATE OUT

DATE BACK

CONDITION OF ITEM

	P	G	F	E
OUT				
BACK				
LOAN TO AGAIN	Y		N	

BORROWER AND INFO

ITEM LOANED

NOTES

DATE OUT

DATE BACK

CONDITION OF ITEM

	P	G	F	E
OUT				
BACK				
LOAN TO AGAIN	Y		N	

KEY FOR CONDITION OF ITEM P=POOR G=GOOD F=FAIR E=EXCELLENT

BORROWER AND INFO	ITEM LOANED

NOTES	CONDITION OF ITEM
DATE OUT DATE BACK	P G F E OUT BACK LOAN TO AGAIN Y N

BORROWER AND INFO	ITEM LOANED

NOTES	CONDITION OF ITEM
DATE OUT DATE BACK	P G F E OUT BACK LOAN TO AGAIN Y N

KEY FOR CONDITION OF ITEM P=POOR G=GOOD F=FAIR E=EXCELLENT

BORROWER AND INFO	ITEM LOANED

NOTES	CONDITION OF ITEM
DATE OUT DATE BACK	P G F E OUT BACK LOAN TO AGAIN Y N

BORROWER AND INFO	ITEM LOANED

NOTES	CONDITION OF ITEM
DATE OUT DATE BACK	P G F E OUT BACK LOAN TO AGAIN Y N

KEY FOR CONDITION OF ITEM P=POOR G=GOOD F=FAIR E=EXCELLENT

BORROWER AND INFO	ITEM LOANED

NOTES	CONDITION OF ITEM
DATE OUT DATE BACK	

	P	G	F	E
OUT				
BACK				

LOAN TO AGAIN	Y		N	

BORROWER AND INFO	ITEM LOANED

NOTES	CONDITION OF ITEM
DATE OUT DATE BACK	

	P	G	F	E
OUT				
BACK				

LOAN TO AGAIN	Y		N	

KEY FOR CONDITION OF ITEM P=POOR G=GOOD F=FAIR E=EXCELLENT

BORROWER AND INFO	ITEM LOANED

NOTES	CONDITION OF ITEM
DATE OUT DATE BACK	P G F E OUT ☐☐☐☐ BACK ☐☐☐☐ LOAN TO AGAIN Y ☐ N ☐

BORROWER AND INFO	ITEM LOANED

NOTES	CONDITION OF ITEM
DATE OUT DATE BACK	P G F E OUT ☐☐☐☐ BACK ☐☐☐☐ LOAN TO AGAIN Y ☐ N ☐

KEY FOR CONDITION OF ITEM P=POOR G=GOOD F=FAIR E=EXCELLENT

BORROWER AND INFO	ITEM LOANED

NOTES	CONDITION OF ITEM
DATE OUT DATE BACK	P G F E OUT BACK LOAN TO AGAIN Y N

BORROWER AND INFO	ITEM LOANED

NOTES	CONDITION OF ITEM
DATE OUT DATE BACK	P G F E OUT BACK LOAN TO AGAIN Y N

KEY FOR CONDITION OF ITEM P=POOR G=GOOD F=FAIR E=EXCELLENT

BORROWER AND INFO	ITEM LOANED

NOTES	CONDITION OF ITEM
DATE OUT DATE BACK	P G F E OUT ☐☐☐☐ BACK ☐☐☐☐ LOAN TO AGAIN Y ☐ N ☐

BORROWER AND INFO	ITEM LOANED

NOTES	CONDITION OF ITEM
DATE OUT DATE BACK	P G F E OUT ☐☐☐☐ BACK ☐☐☐☐ LOAN TO AGAIN Y ☐ N ☐

KEY FOR CONDITION OF ITEM P=POOR G=GOOD F=FAIR E=EXCELLENT

BORROWER AND INFO | ITEM LOANED

NOTES

DATE OUT

DATE BACK

CONDITION OF ITEM

	P	G	F	E
OUT				
BACK				
LOAN TO AGAIN	Y		N	

BORROWER AND INFO | ITEM LOANED

NOTES

DATE OUT

DATE BACK

CONDITION OF ITEM

	P	G	F	E
OUT				
BACK				
LOAN TO AGAIN	Y		N	

KEY FOR CONDITION OF ITEM P=POOR G=GOOD F=FAIR E=EXCELLENT

BORROWER AND INFO	ITEM LOANED

NOTES	CONDITION OF ITEM
DATE OUT DATE BACK	P G F E OUT ☐☐☐☐ BACK ☐☐☐☐ LOAN TO AGAIN Y ☐ N ☐

BORROWER AND INFO	ITEM LOANED

NOTES	CONDITION OF ITEM
DATE OUT DATE BACK	P G F E OUT ☐☐☐☐ BACK ☐☐☐☐ LOAN TO AGAIN Y ☐ N ☐

KEY FOR CONDITION OF ITEM P=POOR G=GOOD F=FAIR E=EXCELLENT

BORROWER AND INFO	ITEM LOANED

NOTES	CONDITION OF ITEM
DATE OUT DATE BACK	P G F E OUT ☐☐☐☐ BACK ☐☐☐☐ LOAN TO AGAIN Y ☐ N ☐

BORROWER AND INFO	ITEM LOANED

NOTES	CONDITION OF ITEM
DATE OUT DATE BACK	P G F E OUT ☐☐☐☐ BACK ☐☐☐☐ LOAN TO AGAIN Y ☐ N ☐

KEY FOR CONDITION OF ITEM P=POOR G=GOOD F=FAIR E=EXCELLENT

BORROWER AND INFO	ITEM LOANED

NOTES	CONDITION OF ITEM				
DATE OUT DATE BACK		P	G	F	E
	OUT				
	BACK				
	LOAN TO AGAIN	Y		N	

BORROWER AND INFO	ITEM LOANED

NOTES	CONDITION OF ITEM				
DATE OUT DATE BACK		P	G	F	E
	OUT				
	BACK				
	LOAN TO AGAIN	Y		N	

KEY FOR CONDITION OF ITEM P=POOR G=GOOD F=FAIR E=EXCELLENT

BORROWER AND INFO	ITEM LOANED

NOTES	CONDITION OF ITEM
DATE OUT DATE BACK	P G F E OUT BACK LOAN TO AGAIN Y N

BORROWER AND INFO	ITEM LOANED

NOTES	CONDITION OF ITEM
DATE OUT DATE BACK	P G F E OUT BACK LOAN TO AGAIN Y N

KEY FOR CONDITION OF ITEM P=POOR G=GOOD F=FAIR E=EXCELLENT

BORROWER AND INFO | **ITEM LOANED**

NOTES

DATE OUT

DATE BACK

CONDITION OF ITEM

	P	G	F	E
OUT				
BACK				

LOAN TO AGAIN	Y		N	

BORROWER AND INFO | **ITEM LOANED**

NOTES

DATE OUT

DATE BACK

CONDITION OF ITEM

	P	G	F	E
OUT				
BACK				

LOAN TO AGAIN	Y		N	

KEY FOR CONDITION OF ITEM P=POOR G=GOOD F=FAIR E=EXCELLENT

BORROWER AND INFO	ITEM LOANED

NOTES	CONDITION OF ITEM
DATE OUT DATE BACK	P G F E OUT ☐☐☐☐ BACK ☐☐☐☐ LOAN TO AGAIN Y ☐ N ☐

BORROWER AND INFO	ITEM LOANED

NOTES	CONDITION OF ITEM
DATE OUT DATE BACK	P G F E OUT ☐☐☐☐ BACK ☐☐☐☐ LOAN TO AGAIN Y ☐ N ☐

KEY FOR CONDITION OF ITEM P=POOR G=GOOD F=FAIR E=EXCELLENT

BORROWER AND INFO	ITEM LOANED

NOTES	CONDITION OF ITEM
DATE OUT DATE BACK	P G F E OUT BACK LOAN TO AGAIN Y N

BORROWER AND INFO	ITEM LOANED

NOTES	CONDITION OF ITEM
DATE OUT DATE BACK	P G F E OUT BACK LOAN TO AGAIN Y N

KEY FOR CONDITION OF ITEM P=POOR G=GOOD F=FAIR E=EXCELLENT

BORROWER AND INFO	ITEM LOANED

NOTES	CONDITION OF ITEM
DATE OUT DATE BACK	P G F E OUT ☐☐☐☐ BACK ☐☐☐☐ LOAN TO AGAIN Y ☐ N ☐

BORROWER AND INFO	ITEM LOANED

NOTES	CONDITION OF ITEM
DATE OUT DATE BACK	P G F E OUT ☐☐☐☐ BACK ☐☐☐☐ LOAN TO AGAIN Y ☐ N ☐

KEY FOR CONDITION OF ITEM P=POOR G=GOOD F=FAIR E=EXCELLENT

BORROWER AND INFO	ITEM LOANED

NOTES	CONDITION OF ITEM
DATE OUT DATE BACK	

	P	G	F	E
OUT				
BACK				
LOAN TO AGAIN	Y		N	

BORROWER AND INFO	ITEM LOANED

NOTES	CONDITION OF ITEM
DATE OUT DATE BACK	

	P	G	F	E
OUT				
BACK				
LOAN TO AGAIN	Y		N	

KEY FOR CONDITION OF ITEM P=POOR G=GOOD F=FAIR E=EXCELLENT

BORROWER AND INFO	ITEM LOANED

NOTES	CONDITION OF ITEM
DATE OUT DATE BACK	P G F E OUT ☐☐☐☐ BACK ☐☐☐☐ LOAN TO AGAIN Y ☐ N ☐

BORROWER AND INFO	ITEM LOANED

NOTES	CONDITION OF ITEM
DATE OUT DATE BACK	P G F E OUT ☐☐☐☐ BACK ☐☐☐☐ LOAN TO AGAIN Y ☐ N ☐

KEY FOR CONDITION OF ITEM P=POOR G=GOOD F=FAIR E=EXCELLENT

BORROWER AND INFO	ITEM LOANED

NOTES	CONDITION OF ITEM
DATE OUT DATE BACK	P G F E OUT ☐☐☐☐ BACK ☐☐☐☐ LOAN TO AGAIN Y ☐ N ☐

BORROWER AND INFO	ITEM LOANED

NOTES	CONDITION OF ITEM
DATE OUT DATE BACK	P G F E OUT ☐☐☐☐ BACK ☐☐☐☐ LOAN TO AGAIN Y ☐ N ☐

KEY FOR CONDITION OF ITEM P=POOR G=GOOD F=FAIR E=EXCELLENT

BORROWER AND INFO	ITEM LOANED

NOTES	CONDITION OF ITEM
DATE OUT DATE BACK	P G F E OUT ☐☐☐☐ BACK ☐☐☐☐ LOAN TO AGAIN Y ☐ N ☐

BORROWER AND INFO	ITEM LOANED

NOTES	CONDITION OF ITEM
DATE OUT DATE BACK	P G F E OUT ☐☐☐☐ BACK ☐☐☐☐ LOAN TO AGAIN Y ☐ N ☐

KEY FOR CONDITION OF ITEM P=POOR G=GOOD F=FAIR E=EXCELLENT

BORROWER AND INFO	ITEM LOANED

NOTES	CONDITION OF ITEM				
DATE OUT DATE BACK		P	G	F	E
	OUT				
	BACK				
	LOAN TO AGAIN	Y		N	

BORROWER AND INFO	ITEM LOANED

NOTES	CONDITION OF ITEM				
DATE OUT DATE BACK		P	G	F	E
	OUT				
	BACK				
	LOAN TO AGAIN	Y		N	

KEY FOR CONDITION OF ITEM P=POOR G=GOOD F=FAIR E=EXCELLENT

BORROWER AND INFO	ITEM LOANED

NOTES	CONDITION OF ITEM
DATE OUT DATE BACK	P G F E OUT BACK LOAN TO AGAIN Y N

BORROWER AND INFO	ITEM LOANED

NOTES	CONDITION OF ITEM
DATE OUT DATE BACK	P G F E OUT BACK LOAN TO AGAIN Y N

KEY FOR CONDITION OF ITEM P=POOR G=GOOD F=FAIR E=EXCELLENT

BORROWER AND INFO	ITEM LOANED

NOTES	CONDITION OF ITEM
DATE OUT DATE BACK	P G F E OUT ☐☐☐☐ BACK ☐☐☐☐ LOAN TO AGAIN Y ☐ N ☐

BORROWER AND INFO	ITEM LOANED

NOTES	CONDITION OF ITEM
DATE OUT DATE BACK	P G F E OUT ☐☐☐☐ BACK ☐☐☐☐ LOAN TO AGAIN Y ☐ N ☐

KEY FOR CONDITION OF ITEM P=POOR G=GOOD F=FAIR E=EXCELLENT

BORROWER AND INFO	ITEM LOANED

NOTES	CONDITION OF ITEM
DATE OUT DATE BACK	P G F E OUT ☐☐☐☐ BACK ☐☐☐☐ LOAN TO AGAIN Y ☐ N ☐

BORROWER AND INFO	ITEM LOANED

NOTES	CONDITION OF ITEM
DATE OUT DATE BACK	P G F E OUT ☐☐☐☐ BACK ☐☐☐☐ LOAN TO AGAIN Y ☐ N ☐

KEY FOR CONDITION OF ITEM P=POOR G=GOOD F=FAIR E=EXCELLENT

BORROWER AND INFO	ITEM LOANED

NOTES	CONDITION OF ITEM
DATE OUT DATE BACK	P G F E OUT BACK LOAN TO AGAIN Y N

BORROWER AND INFO	ITEM LOANED

NOTES	CONDITION OF ITEM
DATE OUT DATE BACK	P G F E OUT BACK LOAN TO AGAIN Y N

KEY FOR CONDITION OF ITEM P=POOR G=GOOD F=FAIR E=EXCELLENT

BORROWER AND INFO	ITEM LOANED

NOTES	CONDITION OF ITEM
DATE OUT DATE BACK	P G F E OUT ☐☐☐☐ BACK ☐☐☐☐ LOAN TO AGAIN Y ☐ N ☐

BORROWER AND INFO	ITEM LOANED

NOTES	CONDITION OF ITEM
DATE OUT DATE BACK	P G F E OUT ☐☐☐☐ BACK ☐☐☐☐ LOAN TO AGAIN Y ☐ N ☐

KEY FOR CONDITION OF ITEM P=POOR G=GOOD F=FAIR E=EXCELLENT

BORROWER AND INFO	ITEM LOANED

NOTES	CONDITION OF ITEM
DATE OUT DATE BACK	

	P	G	F	E
OUT				
BACK				

LOAN TO AGAIN	Y		N	

BORROWER AND INFO	ITEM LOANED

NOTES	CONDITION OF ITEM
DATE OUT DATE BACK	

	P	G	F	E
OUT				
BACK				

LOAN TO AGAIN	Y		N	

KEY FOR CONDITION OF ITEM P=POOR G=GOOD F=FAIR E=EXCELLENT

BORROWER AND INFO	ITEM LOANED

NOTES	CONDITION OF ITEM
DATE OUT DATE BACK	P G F E OUT ☐☐☐☐ BACK ☐☐☐☐ LOAN TO AGAIN Y ☐ N ☐

BORROWER AND INFO	ITEM LOANED

NOTES	CONDITION OF ITEM
DATE OUT DATE BACK	P G F E OUT ☐☐☐☐ BACK ☐☐☐☐ LOAN TO AGAIN Y ☐ N ☐

KEY FOR CONDITION OF ITEM P=POOR G=GOOD F=FAIR E=EXCELLENT

BORROWER AND INFO	ITEM LOANED

NOTES	CONDITION OF ITEM
DATE OUT DATE BACK	P G F E OUT ☐☐☐☐ BACK ☐☐☐☐ LOAN TO AGAIN Y ☐ N ☐

BORROWER AND INFO	ITEM LOANED

NOTES	CONDITION OF ITEM
DATE OUT DATE BACK	P G F E OUT ☐☐☐☐ BACK ☐☐☐☐ LOAN TO AGAIN Y ☐ N ☐

KEY FOR CONDITION OF ITEM P=POOR G=GOOD F=FAIR E=EXCELLENT

BORROWER AND INFO	ITEM LOANED

NOTES	CONDITION OF ITEM
DATE OUT DATE BACK	P G F E OUT ☐☐☐☐ BACK ☐☐☐☐ LOAN TO AGAIN Y ☐ N ☐

BORROWER AND INFO	ITEM LOANED

NOTES	CONDITION OF ITEM
DATE OUT DATE BACK	P G F E OUT ☐☐☐☐ BACK ☐☐☐☐ LOAN TO AGAIN Y ☐ N ☐

KEY FOR CONDITION OF ITEM P=POOR G=GOOD F=FAIR E=EXCELLENT

BORROWER AND INFO	ITEM LOANED

NOTES	CONDITION OF ITEM
DATE OUT DATE BACK	P G F E OUT ☐☐☐☐ BACK ☐☐☐☐ LOAN TO AGAIN Y ☐ N ☐

BORROWER AND INFO	ITEM LOANED

NOTES	CONDITION OF ITEM
DATE OUT DATE BACK	P G F E OUT ☐☐☐☐ BACK ☐☐☐☐ LOAN TO AGAIN Y ☐ N ☐

KEY FOR CONDITION OF ITEM P=POOR G=GOOD F=FAIR E=EXCELLENT

BORROWER AND INFO	ITEM LOANED

NOTES	CONDITION OF ITEM
DATE OUT DATE BACK	P G F E OUT ☐ ☐ ☐ ☐ BACK ☐ ☐ ☐ ☐ LOAN TO AGAIN Y ☐ N ☐

BORROWER AND INFO	ITEM LOANED

NOTES	CONDITION OF ITEM
DATE OUT DATE BACK	P G F E OUT ☐ ☐ ☐ ☐ BACK ☐ ☐ ☐ ☐ LOAN TO AGAIN Y ☐ N ☐

KEY FOR CONDITION OF ITEM P=POOR G=GOOD F=FAIR E=EXCELLENT

BORROWER AND INFO

ITEM LOANED

NOTES

DATE OUT

DATE BACK

CONDITION OF ITEM

	P	G	F	E
OUT				
BACK				

LOAN TO AGAIN Y N

BORROWER AND INFO

ITEM LOANED

NOTES

DATE OUT

DATE BACK

CONDITION OF ITEM

	P	G	F	E
OUT				
BACK				

LOAN TO AGAIN Y N

KEY FOR CONDITION OF ITEM P=POOR G=GOOD F=FAIR E=EXCELLENT

BORROWER AND INFO	ITEM LOANED

NOTES	CONDITION OF ITEM
DATE OUT DATE BACK	P G F E OUT BACK LOAN TO AGAIN Y N

BORROWER AND INFO	ITEM LOANED

NOTES	CONDITION OF ITEM
DATE OUT DATE BACK	P G F E OUT BACK LOAN TO AGAIN Y N

KEY FOR CONDITION OF ITEM P=POOR G=GOOD F=FAIR E=EXCELLENT

BORROWER AND INFO	ITEM LOANED

NOTES	CONDITION OF ITEM
DATE OUT DATE BACK	

	P	G	F	E
OUT				
BACK				
LOAN TO AGAIN	Y		N	

BORROWER AND INFO	ITEM LOANED

NOTES	CONDITION OF ITEM
DATE OUT DATE BACK	

	P	G	F	E
OUT				
BACK				
LOAN TO AGAIN	Y		N	

KEY FOR CONDITION OF ITEM P=POOR G=GOOD F=FAIR E=EXCELLENT

BORROWER AND INFO	ITEM LOANED

NOTES	CONDITION OF ITEM
DATE OUT DATE BACK	P G F E OUT ☐☐☐☐ BACK ☐☐☐☐ LOAN TO AGAIN Y ☐ N ☐

BORROWER AND INFO	ITEM LOANED

NOTES	CONDITION OF ITEM
DATE OUT DATE BACK	P G F E OUT ☐☐☐☐ BACK ☐☐☐☐ LOAN TO AGAIN Y ☐ N ☐

KEY FOR CONDITION OF ITEM P=POOR G=GOOD F=FAIR E=EXCELLENT

BORROWER AND INFO	ITEM LOANED

NOTES	CONDITION OF ITEM
DATE OUT DATE BACK	P G F E OUT ☐☐☐☐ BACK ☐☐☐☐ LOAN TO AGAIN Y ☐ N ☐

BORROWER AND INFO	ITEM LOANED

NOTES	CONDITION OF ITEM
DATE OUT DATE BACK	P G F E OUT ☐☐☐☐ BACK ☐☐☐☐ LOAN TO AGAIN Y ☐ N ☐

KEY FOR CONDITION OF ITEM P=POOR G=GOOD F=FAIR E=EXCELLENT

BORROWER AND INFO	ITEM LOANED

NOTES	CONDITION OF ITEM
DATE OUT DATE BACK	P G F E OUT ☐ ☐ ☐ ☐ BACK ☐ ☐ ☐ ☐ LOAN TO AGAIN Y ☐ N ☐

BORROWER AND INFO	ITEM LOANED

NOTES	CONDITION OF ITEM
DATE OUT DATE BACK	P G F E OUT ☐ ☐ ☐ ☐ BACK ☐ ☐ ☐ ☐ LOAN TO AGAIN Y ☐ N ☐

KEY FOR CONDITION OF ITEM P=POOR G=GOOD F=FAIR E=EXCELLENT

BORROWER AND INFO	ITEM LOANED

NOTES	CONDITION OF ITEM
DATE OUT DATE BACK	P G F E OUT BACK LOAN TO AGAIN Y N

BORROWER AND INFO	ITEM LOANED

NOTES	CONDITION OF ITEM
DATE OUT DATE BACK	P G F E OUT BACK LOAN TO AGAIN Y N

KEY FOR CONDITION OF ITEM P=POOR G=GOOD F=FAIR E=EXCELLENT

BORROWER AND INFO	ITEM LOANED

NOTES	CONDITION OF ITEM
DATE OUT DATE BACK	P G F E OUT ☐☐☐☐ BACK ☐☐☐☐ LOAN TO AGAIN Y ☐ N ☐

BORROWER AND INFO	ITEM LOANED

NOTES	CONDITION OF ITEM
DATE OUT DATE BACK	P G F E OUT ☐☐☐☐ BACK ☐☐☐☐ LOAN TO AGAIN Y ☐ N ☐

KEY FOR CONDITION OF ITEM P=POOR G=GOOD F=FAIR E=EXCELLENT

BORROWER AND INFO	ITEM LOANED

NOTES	CONDITION OF ITEM
DATE OUT DATE BACK	P G F E OUT ☐ ☐ ☐ ☐ BACK ☐ ☐ ☐ ☐ LOAN TO AGAIN Y ☐ N ☐

BORROWER AND INFO	ITEM LOANED

NOTES	CONDITION OF ITEM
DATE OUT DATE BACK	P G F E OUT ☐ ☐ ☐ ☐ BACK ☐ ☐ ☐ ☐ LOAN TO AGAIN Y ☐ N ☐

KEY FOR CONDITION OF ITEM P=POOR G=GOOD F=FAIR E=EXCELLENT

BORROWER AND INFO	ITEM LOANED

NOTES	CONDITION OF ITEM
DATE OUT DATE BACK	P G F E OUT ☐☐☐☐ BACK ☐☐☐☐ LOAN TO AGAIN Y ☐ N ☐

BORROWER AND INFO	ITEM LOANED

NOTES	CONDITION OF ITEM
DATE OUT DATE BACK	P G F E OUT ☐☐☐☐ BACK ☐☐☐☐ LOAN TO AGAIN Y ☐ N ☐

KEY FOR CONDITION OF ITEM P=POOR G=GOOD F=FAIR E=EXCELLENT

BORROWER AND INFO	ITEM LOANED

NOTES	CONDITION OF ITEM
DATE OUT DATE BACK	P G F E OUT ☐☐☐☐ BACK ☐☐☐☐ LOAN TO AGAIN Y ☐ N ☐

BORROWER AND INFO	ITEM LOANED

NOTES	CONDITION OF ITEM
DATE OUT DATE BACK	P G F E OUT ☐☐☐☐ BACK ☐☐☐☐ LOAN TO AGAIN Y ☐ N ☐

KEY FOR CONDITION OF ITEM P=POOR G=GOOD F=FAIR E=EXCELLENT

BORROWER AND INFO	ITEM LOANED

NOTES	CONDITION OF ITEM
DATE OUT DATE BACK	P G F E OUT ☐☐☐☐ BACK ☐☐☐☐ LOAN TO AGAIN Y ☐ N ☐

BORROWER AND INFO	ITEM LOANED

NOTES	CONDITION OF ITEM
DATE OUT DATE BACK	P G F E OUT ☐☐☐☐ BACK ☐☐☐☐ LOAN TO AGAIN Y ☐ N ☐

KEY FOR CONDITION OF ITEM P=POOR G=GOOD F=FAIR E=EXCELLENT

BORROWER AND INFO

ITEM LOANED

NOTES

DATE OUT

DATE BACK

CONDITION OF ITEM

	P	G	F	E
OUT				
BACK				
LOAN TO AGAIN	Y		N	

BORROWER AND INFO

ITEM LOANED

NOTES

DATE OUT

DATE BACK

CONDITION OF ITEM

	P	G	F	E
OUT				
BACK				
LOAN TO AGAIN	Y		N	

KEY FOR CONDITION OF ITEM P=POOR G=GOOD F=FAIR E=EXCELLENT

BORROWER AND INFO	ITEM LOANED

NOTES	CONDITION OF ITEM
DATE OUT DATE BACK	P G F E OUT ☐☐☐☐ BACK ☐☐☐☐ LOAN TO AGAIN Y ☐ N ☐

BORROWER AND INFO	ITEM LOANED

NOTES	CONDITION OF ITEM
DATE OUT DATE BACK	P G F E OUT ☐☐☐☐ BACK ☐☐☐☐ LOAN TO AGAIN Y ☐ N ☐

KEY FOR CONDITION OF ITEM P=POOR G=GOOD F=FAIR E=EXCELLENT

BORROWER AND INFO	ITEM LOANED

NOTES	CONDITION OF ITEM
DATE OUT DATE BACK	

	P	G	F	E
OUT				
BACK				
LOAN TO AGAIN	Y		N	

BORROWER AND INFO	ITEM LOANED

NOTES	CONDITION OF ITEM
DATE OUT DATE BACK	

	P	G	F	E
OUT				
BACK				
LOAN TO AGAIN	Y		N	

KEY FOR CONDITION OF ITEM P=POOR G=GOOD F=FAIR E=EXCELLENT

BORROWER AND INFO	ITEM LOANED

NOTES	CONDITION OF ITEM
DATE OUT DATE BACK	

	P	G	F	E
OUT				
BACK				
LOAN TO AGAIN	Y		N	

BORROWER AND INFO	ITEM LOANED

NOTES	CONDITION OF ITEM
DATE OUT DATE BACK	

	P	G	F	E
OUT				
BACK				
LOAN TO AGAIN	Y		N	

KEY FOR CONDITION OF ITEM P=POOR G=GOOD F=FAIR E=EXCELLENT

BORROWER AND INFO	ITEM LOANED

NOTES	CONDITION OF ITEM
DATE OUT DATE BACK	

	P	G	F	E
OUT				
BACK				
LOAN TO AGAIN	Y		N	

BORROWER AND INFO	ITEM LOANED

NOTES	CONDITION OF ITEM
DATE OUT DATE BACK	

	P	G	F	E
OUT				
BACK				
LOAN TO AGAIN	Y		N	

KEY FOR CONDITION OF ITEM P=POOR G=GOOD F=FAIR E=EXCELLENT

BORROWER AND INFO	ITEM LOANED

NOTES	CONDITION OF ITEM
DATE OUT DATE BACK	

	P	G	F	E
OUT				
BACK				
LOAN TO AGAIN	Y		N	

BORROWER AND INFO	ITEM LOANED

NOTES	CONDITION OF ITEM
DATE OUT DATE BACK	

	P	G	F	E
OUT				
BACK				
LOAN TO AGAIN	Y		N	

KEY FOR CONDITION OF ITEM P=POOR G=GOOD F=FAIR E=EXCELLENT

BORROWER AND INFO | **ITEM LOANED**

NOTES

DATE OUT

DATE BACK

CONDITION OF ITEM

	P	G	F	E
OUT				
BACK				
LOAN TO AGAIN	Y		N	

BORROWER AND INFO | **ITEM LOANED**

NOTES

DATE OUT

DATE BACK

CONDITION OF ITEM

	P	G	F	E
OUT				
BACK				
LOAN TO AGAIN	Y		N	

KEY FOR CONDITION OF ITEM P=POOR G=GOOD F=FAIR E=EXCELLENT

BORROWER AND INFO	ITEM LOANED

NOTES	CONDITION OF ITEM
DATE OUT DATE BACK	P G F E OUT ☐☐☐☐ BACK ☐☐☐☐ LOAN TO AGAIN Y ☐ N ☐

BORROWER AND INFO	ITEM LOANED

NOTES	CONDITION OF ITEM
DATE OUT DATE BACK	P G F E OUT ☐☐☐☐ BACK ☐☐☐☐ LOAN TO AGAIN Y ☐ N ☐

KEY FOR CONDITION OF ITEM P=POOR G=GOOD F=FAIR E=EXCELLENT

BORROWER AND INFO

ITEM LOANED

NOTES

DATE OUT

DATE BACK

CONDITION OF ITEM

	P	G	F	E
OUT				
BACK				

LOAN TO AGAIN Y N

BORROWER AND INFO

ITEM LOANED

NOTES

DATE OUT

DATE BACK

CONDITION OF ITEM

	P	G	F	E
OUT				
BACK				

LOAN TO AGAIN Y N

KEY FOR CONDITION OF ITEM P=POOR G=GOOD F=FAIR E=EXCELLENT

BORROWER AND INFO	ITEM LOANED

NOTES	CONDITION OF ITEM
DATE OUT DATE BACK	P G F E OUT ☐☐☐☐ BACK ☐☐☐☐ LOAN TO AGAIN Y ☐ N ☐

BORROWER AND INFO	ITEM LOANED

NOTES	CONDITION OF ITEM
DATE OUT DATE BACK	P G F E OUT ☐☐☐☐ BACK ☐☐☐☐ LOAN TO AGAIN Y ☐ N ☐

KEY FOR CONDITION OF ITEM P=POOR G=GOOD F=FAIR E=EXCELLENT

BORROWER AND INFO	ITEM LOANED

NOTES	CONDITION OF ITEM
DATE OUT DATE BACK	P G F E OUT ☐☐☐☐ BACK ☐☐☐☐ LOAN TO AGAIN Y ☐ N ☐

BORROWER AND INFO	ITEM LOANED

NOTES	CONDITION OF ITEM
DATE OUT DATE BACK	P G F E OUT ☐☐☐☐ BACK ☐☐☐☐ LOAN TO AGAIN Y ☐ N ☐

KEY FOR CONDITION OF ITEM P=POOR G=GOOD F=FAIR E=EXCELLENT

BORROWER AND INFO	ITEM LOANED

NOTES	CONDITION OF ITEM
DATE OUT DATE BACK	P G F E OUT ☐☐☐☐ BACK ☐☐☐☐ LOAN TO AGAIN Y ☐ N ☐

BORROWER AND INFO	ITEM LOANED

NOTES	CONDITION OF ITEM
DATE OUT DATE BACK	P G F E OUT ☐☐☐☐ BACK ☐☐☐☐ LOAN TO AGAIN Y ☐ N ☐

KEY FOR CONDITION OF ITEM P=POOR G=GOOD F=FAIR E=EXCELLENT

BORROWER AND INFO	ITEM LOANED

NOTES	CONDITION OF ITEM
DATE OUT DATE BACK	P G F E OUT ☐ ☐ ☐ ☐ BACK ☐ ☐ ☐ ☐ LOAN TO AGAIN Y ☐ N ☐

BORROWER AND INFO	ITEM LOANED

NOTES	CONDITION OF ITEM
DATE OUT DATE BACK	P G F E OUT ☐ ☐ ☐ ☐ BACK ☐ ☐ ☐ ☐ LOAN TO AGAIN Y ☐ N ☐

KEY FOR CONDITION OF ITEM P=POOR G=GOOD F=FAIR E=EXCELLENT

BORROWER AND INFO	ITEM LOANED

NOTES	CONDITION OF ITEM
DATE OUT DATE BACK	P G F E OUT ☐☐☐☐ BACK ☐☐☐☐ LOAN TO AGAIN Y ☐ N ☐

BORROWER AND INFO	ITEM LOANED

NOTES	CONDITION OF ITEM
DATE OUT DATE BACK	P G F E OUT ☐☐☐☐ BACK ☐☐☐☐ LOAN TO AGAIN Y ☐ N ☐

KEY FOR CONDITION OF ITEM P=POOR G=GOOD F=FAIR E=EXCELLENT

BORROWER AND INFO	ITEM LOANED

NOTES	CONDITION OF ITEM
DATE OUT DATE BACK	P G F E OUT ☐☐☐☐ BACK ☐☐☐☐ LOAN TO AGAIN Y ☐ N ☐

BORROWER AND INFO	ITEM LOANED

NOTES	CONDITION OF ITEM
DATE OUT DATE BACK	P G F E OUT ☐☐☐☐ BACK ☐☐☐☐ LOAN TO AGAIN Y ☐ N ☐

KEY FOR CONDITION OF ITEM P=POOR G=GOOD F=FAIR E=EXCELLENT

BORROWER AND INFO	ITEM LOANED

NOTES	CONDITION OF ITEM
DATE OUT DATE BACK	P G F E OUT □ □ □ □ BACK □ □ □ □ LOAN TO AGAIN Y □ N □

BORROWER AND INFO	ITEM LOANED

NOTES	CONDITION OF ITEM
DATE OUT DATE BACK	P G F E OUT □ □ □ □ BACK □ □ □ □ LOAN TO AGAIN Y □ N □

KEY FOR CONDITION OF ITEM P=POOR G=GOOD F=FAIR E=EXCELLENT

BORROWER AND INFO	ITEM LOANED

NOTES	CONDITION OF ITEM
DATE OUT DATE BACK	P G F E OUT BACK LOAN TO AGAIN Y N

BORROWER AND INFO	ITEM LOANED

NOTES	CONDITION OF ITEM
DATE OUT DATE BACK	P G F E OUT BACK LOAN TO AGAIN Y N

KEY FOR CONDITION OF ITEM P=POOR G=GOOD F=FAIR E=EXCELLENT

BORROWER AND INFO	ITEM LOANED

NOTES	CONDITION OF ITEM
DATE OUT DATE BACK	

	P	G	F	E
OUT				
BACK				
LOAN TO AGAIN	Y		N	

BORROWER AND INFO	ITEM LOANED

NOTES	CONDITION OF ITEM
DATE OUT DATE BACK	

	P	G	F	E
OUT				
BACK				
LOAN TO AGAIN	Y		N	

KEY FOR CONDITION OF ITEM P=POOR G=GOOD F=FAIR E=EXCELLENT

BORROWER AND INFO	ITEM LOANED

NOTES	CONDITION OF ITEM
DATE OUT DATE BACK	P G F E OUT BACK LOAN TO AGAIN Y N

BORROWER AND INFO	ITEM LOANED

NOTES	CONDITION OF ITEM
DATE OUT DATE BACK	P G F E OUT BACK LOAN TO AGAIN Y N

KEY FOR CONDITION OF ITEM P=POOR G=GOOD F=FAIR E=EXCELLENT

BORROWER AND INFO	ITEM LOANED

NOTES	CONDITION OF ITEM
DATE OUT DATE BACK	P G F E OUT BACK LOAN TO AGAIN Y N

BORROWER AND INFO	ITEM LOANED

NOTES	CONDITION OF ITEM
DATE OUT DATE BACK	P G F E OUT BACK LOAN TO AGAIN Y N

KEY FOR CONDITION OF ITEM P=POOR G=GOOD F=FAIR E=EXCELLENT

BORROWER AND INFO	ITEM LOANED

NOTES	CONDITION OF ITEM
DATE OUT DATE BACK	P G F E OUT ☐☐☐☐ BACK ☐☐☐☐ LOAN TO AGAIN Y ☐ N ☐

BORROWER AND INFO	ITEM LOANED

NOTES	CONDITION OF ITEM
DATE OUT DATE BACK	P G F E OUT ☐☐☐☐ BACK ☐☐☐☐ LOAN TO AGAIN Y ☐ N ☐

KEY FOR CONDITION OF ITEM P=POOR G=GOOD F=FAIR E=EXCELLENT

BORROWER AND INFO	ITEM LOANED

NOTES	CONDITION OF ITEM
DATE OUT DATE BACK	P G F E OUT ☐☐☐☐ BACK ☐☐☐☐ LOAN TO AGAIN Y ☐ N ☐

BORROWER AND INFO	ITEM LOANED

NOTES	CONDITION OF ITEM
DATE OUT DATE BACK	P G F E OUT ☐☐☐☐ BACK ☐☐☐☐ LOAN TO AGAIN Y ☐ N ☐

KEY FOR CONDITION OF ITEM P=POOR G=GOOD F=FAIR E=EXCELLENT

BORROWER AND INFO

ITEM LOANED

NOTES

DATE OUT

DATE BACK

CONDITION OF ITEM

	P	G	F	E
OUT				
BACK				
LOAN TO AGAIN	Y		N	

BORROWER AND INFO

ITEM LOANED

NOTES

DATE OUT

DATE BACK

CONDITION OF ITEM

	P	G	F	E
OUT				
BACK				
LOAN TO AGAIN	Y		N	

KEY FOR CONDITION OF ITEM P=POOR G=GOOD F=FAIR E=EXCELLENT

BORROWER AND INFO	ITEM LOANED

NOTES	CONDITION OF ITEM
DATE OUT DATE BACK	P G F E OUT ☐☐☐☐ BACK ☐☐☐☐ LOAN TO AGAIN Y ☐ N ☐

BORROWER AND INFO	ITEM LOANED

NOTES	CONDITION OF ITEM
DATE OUT DATE BACK	P G F E OUT ☐☐☐☐ BACK ☐☐☐☐ LOAN TO AGAIN Y ☐ N ☐

KEY FOR CONDITION OF ITEM P=POOR G=GOOD F=FAIR E=EXCELLENT

BORROWER AND INFO	ITEM LOANED

NOTES	CONDITION OF ITEM
DATE OUT DATE BACK	P G F E OUT BACK LOAN TO AGAIN Y N

BORROWER AND INFO	ITEM LOANED

NOTES	CONDITION OF ITEM
DATE OUT DATE BACK	P G F E OUT BACK LOAN TO AGAIN Y N

KEY FOR CONDITION OF ITEM P=POOR G=GOOD F=FAIR E=EXCELLENT

BORROWER AND INFO	ITEM LOANED

NOTES	CONDITION OF ITEM
DATE OUT DATE BACK	P G F E OUT ☐☐☐☐ BACK ☐☐☐☐ LOAN TO AGAIN Y ☐ N ☐

BORROWER AND INFO	ITEM LOANED

NOTES	CONDITION OF ITEM
DATE OUT DATE BACK	P G F E OUT ☐☐☐☐ BACK ☐☐☐☐ LOAN TO AGAIN Y ☐ N ☐

KEY FOR CONDITION OF ITEM P=POOR G=GOOD F=FAIR E=EXCELLENT

BORROWER AND INFO	ITEM LOANED

NOTES	CONDITION OF ITEM
DATE OUT DATE BACK	P G F E OUT ☐☐☐☐ BACK ☐☐☐☐ LOAN TO AGAIN Y ☐ N ☐

BORROWER AND INFO	ITEM LOANED

NOTES	CONDITION OF ITEM
DATE OUT DATE BACK	P G F E OUT ☐☐☐☐ BACK ☐☐☐☐ LOAN TO AGAIN Y ☐ N ☐

KEY FOR CONDITION OF ITEM P=POOR G=GOOD F=FAIR E=EXCELLENT

BORROWER AND INFO	ITEM LOANED

NOTES	CONDITION OF ITEM
DATE OUT DATE BACK	P G F E OUT BACK LOAN TO AGAIN Y N

BORROWER AND INFO	ITEM LOANED

NOTES	CONDITION OF ITEM
DATE OUT DATE BACK	P G F E OUT BACK LOAN TO AGAIN Y N

KEY FOR CONDITION OF ITEM P=POOR G=GOOD F=FAIR E=EXCELLENT

BORROWER AND INFO	ITEM LOANED

NOTES	CONDITION OF ITEM
DATE OUT DATE BACK	

	P	G	F	E
OUT				
BACK				
LOAN TO AGAIN	Y		N	

BORROWER AND INFO	ITEM LOANED

NOTES	CONDITION OF ITEM
DATE OUT DATE BACK	

	P	G	F	E
OUT				
BACK				
LOAN TO AGAIN	Y		N	

KEY FOR CONDITION OF ITEM P=POOR G=GOOD F=FAIR E=EXCELLENT

BORROWER AND INFO	ITEM LOANED

NOTES	CONDITION OF ITEM
DATE OUT DATE BACK	P G F E OUT ☐☐☐☐ BACK ☐☐☐☐ LOAN TO AGAIN Y ☐ N ☐

BORROWER AND INFO	ITEM LOANED

NOTES	CONDITION OF ITEM
DATE OUT DATE BACK	P G F E OUT ☐☐☐☐ BACK ☐☐☐☐ LOAN TO AGAIN Y ☐ N ☐

KEY FOR CONDITION OF ITEM P=POOR G=GOOD F=FAIR E=EXCELLENT

BORROWER AND INFO	ITEM LOANED

NOTES	CONDITION OF ITEM				
DATE OUT		P	G	F	E
DATE BACK	OUT				
	BACK				
	LOAN TO AGAIN	Y		N	

BORROWER AND INFO	ITEM LOANED

NOTES	CONDITION OF ITEM				
DATE OUT		P	G	F	E
DATE BACK	OUT				
	BACK				
	LOAN TO AGAIN	Y		N	

KEY FOR CONDITION OF ITEM P=POOR G=GOOD F=FAIR E=EXCELLENT

BORROWER AND INFO | ITEM LOANED

NOTES

DATE OUT

DATE BACK

CONDITION OF ITEM

	P	G	F	E
OUT				
BACK				
LOAN TO AGAIN	Y		N	

BORROWER AND INFO | ITEM LOANED

NOTES

DATE OUT

DATE BACK

CONDITION OF ITEM

	P	G	F	E
OUT				
BACK				
LOAN TO AGAIN	Y		N	

KEY FOR CONDITION OF ITEM P=POOR G=GOOD F=FAIR E=EXCELLENT

BORROWER AND INFO	ITEM LOANED

NOTES	CONDITION OF ITEM
DATE OUT DATE BACK	

	P	G	F	E
OUT				
BACK				
LOAN TO AGAIN	Y		N	

BORROWER AND INFO	ITEM LOANED

NOTES	CONDITION OF ITEM
DATE OUT DATE BACK	

	P	G	F	E
OUT				
BACK				
LOAN TO AGAIN	Y		N	

KEY FOR CONDITION OF ITEM P=POOR G=GOOD F=FAIR E=EXCELLENT

BORROWER AND INFO

ITEM LOANED

NOTES

DATE OUT

DATE BACK

CONDITION OF ITEM

	P	G	F	E
OUT				
BACK				

LOAN TO AGAIN Y N

BORROWER AND INFO

ITEM LOANED

NOTES

DATE OUT

DATE BACK

CONDITION OF ITEM

	P	G	F	E
OUT				
BACK				

LOAN TO AGAIN Y N

KEY FOR CONDITION OF ITEM P=POOR G=GOOD F=FAIR E=EXCELLENT

BORROWER AND INFO	ITEM LOANED

NOTES	CONDITION OF ITEM
DATE OUT DATE BACK	

	P	G	F	E
OUT				
BACK				
LOAN TO AGAIN	Y		N	

BORROWER AND INFO	ITEM LOANED

NOTES	CONDITION OF ITEM
DATE OUT DATE BACK	

	P	G	F	E
OUT				
BACK				
LOAN TO AGAIN	Y		N	

KEY FOR CONDITION OF ITEM P=POOR G=GOOD F=FAIR E=EXCELLENT

BORROWER AND INFO	ITEM LOANED

NOTES	CONDITION OF ITEM
DATE OUT DATE BACK	P G F E OUT BACK LOAN TO AGAIN Y N

BORROWER AND INFO	ITEM LOANED

NOTES	CONDITION OF ITEM
DATE OUT DATE BACK	P G F E OUT BACK LOAN TO AGAIN Y N

KEY FOR CONDITION OF ITEM P=POOR G=GOOD F=FAIR E=EXCELLENT

BORROWER AND INFO	ITEM LOANED

NOTES	CONDITION OF ITEM
DATE OUT DATE BACK	P G F E OUT ☐☐☐☐ BACK ☐☐☐☐ LOAN TO AGAIN Y ☐ N ☐

BORROWER AND INFO	ITEM LOANED

NOTES	CONDITION OF ITEM
DATE OUT DATE BACK	P G F E OUT ☐☐☐☐ BACK ☐☐☐☐ LOAN TO AGAIN Y ☐ N ☐

KEY FOR CONDITION OF ITEM P=POOR G=GOOD F=FAIR E=EXCELLENT

BORROWER AND INFO | ITEM LOANED

NOTES

DATE OUT

DATE BACK

CONDITION OF ITEM

	P	G	F	E
OUT				
BACK				
LOAN TO AGAIN	Y		N	

BORROWER AND INFO | ITEM LOANED

NOTES

DATE OUT

DATE BACK

CONDITION OF ITEM

	P	G	F	E
OUT				
BACK				
LOAN TO AGAIN	Y		N	

KEY FOR CONDITION OF ITEM P=POOR G=GOOD F=FAIR E=EXCELLENT

BORROWER AND INFO	ITEM LOANED

NOTES	CONDITION OF ITEM
DATE OUT DATE BACK	P G F E OUT ☐☐☐☐ BACK ☐☐☐☐ LOAN TO AGAIN Y ☐ N ☐

BORROWER AND INFO	ITEM LOANED

NOTES	CONDITION OF ITEM
DATE OUT DATE BACK	P G F E OUT ☐☐☐☐ BACK ☐☐☐☐ LOAN TO AGAIN Y ☐ N ☐

KEY FOR CONDITION OF ITEM P=POOR G=GOOD F=FAIR E=EXCELLENT

BORROWER AND INFO	ITEM LOANED

NOTES	CONDITION OF ITEM
DATE OUT DATE BACK	P G F E OUT ☐ ☐ ☐ ☐ BACK ☐ ☐ ☐ ☐ LOAN TO AGAIN Y ☐ N ☐

BORROWER AND INFO	ITEM LOANED

NOTES	CONDITION OF ITEM
DATE OUT DATE BACK	P G F E OUT ☐ ☐ ☐ ☐ BACK ☐ ☐ ☐ ☐ LOAN TO AGAIN Y ☐ N ☐

KEY FOR CONDITION OF ITEM P=POOR G=GOOD F=FAIR E=EXCELLENT

BORROWER AND INFO	ITEM LOANED

NOTES	CONDITION OF ITEM
DATE OUT DATE BACK	P G F E OUT BACK LOAN TO AGAIN Y N

BORROWER AND INFO	ITEM LOANED

NOTES	CONDITION OF ITEM
DATE OUT DATE BACK	P G F E OUT BACK LOAN TO AGAIN Y N

KEY FOR CONDITION OF ITEM P=POOR G=GOOD F=FAIR E=EXCELLENT

BORROWER AND INFO	ITEM LOANED

NOTES	CONDITION OF ITEM
DATE OUT DATE BACK	P G F E OUT BACK LOAN TO AGAIN Y N

BORROWER AND INFO	ITEM LOANED

NOTES	CONDITION OF ITEM
DATE OUT DATE BACK	P G F E OUT BACK LOAN TO AGAIN Y N

KEY FOR CONDITION OF ITEM P=POOR G=GOOD F=FAIR E=EXCELLENT

BORROWER AND INFO

ITEM LOANED

NOTES

DATE OUT

DATE BACK

CONDITION OF ITEM

	P	G	F	E
OUT				
BACK				

LOAN TO AGAIN	Y	N

BORROWER AND INFO

ITEM LOANED

NOTES

DATE OUT

DATE BACK

CONDITION OF ITEM

	P	G	F	E
OUT				
BACK				

LOAN TO AGAIN	Y	N

KEY FOR CONDITION OF ITEM P=POOR G=GOOD F=FAIR E=EXCELLENT

BORROWER AND INFO	ITEM LOANED

NOTES	CONDITION OF ITEM
DATE OUT DATE BACK	P G F E OUT ☐☐☐☐ BACK ☐☐☐☐ LOAN TO AGAIN Y ☐ N ☐

BORROWER AND INFO	ITEM LOANED

NOTES	CONDITION OF ITEM
DATE OUT DATE BACK	P G F E OUT ☐☐☐☐ BACK ☐☐☐☐ LOAN TO AGAIN Y ☐ N ☐

KEY FOR CONDITION OF ITEM P=POOR G=GOOD F=FAIR E=EXCELLENT

BORROWER AND INFO	ITEM LOANED

NOTES	CONDITION OF ITEM
DATE OUT DATE BACK	P G F E OUT BACK LOAN TO AGAIN Y N

BORROWER AND INFO	ITEM LOANED

NOTES	CONDITION OF ITEM
DATE OUT DATE BACK	P G F E OUT BACK LOAN TO AGAIN Y N

KEY FOR CONDITION OF ITEM P=POOR G=GOOD F=FAIR E=EXCELLENT

BORROWER AND INFO	ITEM LOANED

NOTES	CONDITION OF ITEM
DATE OUT DATE BACK	P G F E OUT ☐☐☐☐ BACK ☐☐☐☐ LOAN TO AGAIN Y ☐ N ☐

BORROWER AND INFO	ITEM LOANED

NOTES	CONDITION OF ITEM
DATE OUT DATE BACK	P G F E OUT ☐☐☐☐ BACK ☐☐☐☐ LOAN TO AGAIN Y ☐ N ☐

KEY FOR CONDITION OF ITEM P=POOR G=GOOD F=FAIR E=EXCELLENT

BORROWER AND INFO	ITEM LOANED

NOTES	CONDITION OF ITEM
DATE OUT DATE BACK	P G F E OUT ☐☐☐☐ BACK ☐☐☐☐ LOAN TO AGAIN Y ☐ N ☐

BORROWER AND INFO	ITEM LOANED

NOTES	CONDITION OF ITEM
DATE OUT DATE BACK	P G F E OUT ☐☐☐☐ BACK ☐☐☐☐ LOAN TO AGAIN Y ☐ N ☐

KEY FOR CONDITION OF ITEM P=POOR G=GOOD F=FAIR E=EXCELLENT

BORROWER AND INFO	ITEM LOANED

NOTES	CONDITION OF ITEM
DATE OUT DATE BACK	P G F E OUT ☐☐☐☐ BACK ☐☐☐☐ LOAN TO AGAIN Y ☐ N ☐

BORROWER AND INFO	ITEM LOANED

NOTES	CONDITION OF ITEM
DATE OUT DATE BACK	P G F E OUT ☐☐☐☐ BACK ☐☐☐☐ LOAN TO AGAIN Y ☐ N ☐

KEY FOR CONDITION OF ITEM P=POOR G=GOOD F=FAIR E=EXCELLENT

BORROWER AND INFO

ITEM LOANED

NOTES

DATE OUT

DATE BACK

CONDITION OF ITEM

	P	G	F	E
OUT				
BACK				
LOAN TO AGAIN	Y		N	

BORROWER AND INFO

ITEM LOANED

NOTES

DATE OUT

DATE BACK

CONDITION OF ITEM

	P	G	F	E
OUT				
BACK				
LOAN TO AGAIN	Y		N	

KEY FOR CONDITION OF ITEM P=POOR G=GOOD F=FAIR E=EXCELLENT

BORROWER AND INFO	ITEM LOANED

NOTES	CONDITION OF ITEM
DATE OUT DATE BACK	P G F E OUT BACK LOAN TO AGAIN Y N

BORROWER AND INFO	ITEM LOANED

NOTES	CONDITION OF ITEM
DATE OUT DATE BACK	P G F E OUT BACK LOAN TO AGAIN Y N

KEY FOR CONDITION OF ITEM P=POOR G=GOOD F=FAIR E=EXCELLENT

BORROWER AND INFO	ITEM LOANED

NOTES	CONDITION OF ITEM
DATE OUT DATE BACK	P G F E OUT ☐☐☐☐ BACK ☐☐☐☐ LOAN TO AGAIN Y ☐ N ☐

BORROWER AND INFO	ITEM LOANED

NOTES	CONDITION OF ITEM
DATE OUT DATE BACK	P G F E OUT ☐☐☐☐ BACK ☐☐☐☐ LOAN TO AGAIN Y ☐ N ☐

KEY FOR CONDITION OF ITEM P=POOR G=GOOD F=FAIR E=EXCELLENT

BORROWER AND INFO	ITEM LOANED

NOTES	CONDITION OF ITEM
DATE OUT DATE BACK	P G F E OUT BACK LOAN TO AGAIN Y N

BORROWER AND INFO	ITEM LOANED

NOTES	CONDITION OF ITEM
DATE OUT DATE BACK	P G F E OUT BACK LOAN TO AGAIN Y N

KEY FOR CONDITION OF ITEM P=POOR G=GOOD F=FAIR E=EXCELLENT

BORROWER AND INFO	ITEM LOANED

NOTES	CONDITION OF ITEM
DATE OUT DATE BACK	P G F E OUT BACK LOAN TO AGAIN Y N

BORROWER AND INFO	ITEM LOANED

NOTES	CONDITION OF ITEM
DATE OUT DATE BACK	P G F E OUT BACK LOAN TO AGAIN Y N

KEY FOR CONDITION OF ITEM P=POOR G=GOOD F=FAIR E=EXCELLENT

BORROWER AND INFO	ITEM LOANED

NOTES	CONDITION OF ITEM
DATE OUT DATE BACK	P G F E OUT ☐☐☐☐ BACK ☐☐☐☐ LOAN TO AGAIN Y ☐ N ☐

BORROWER AND INFO	ITEM LOANED

NOTES	CONDITION OF ITEM
DATE OUT DATE BACK	P G F E OUT ☐☐☐☐ BACK ☐☐☐☐ LOAN TO AGAIN Y ☐ N ☐

KEY FOR CONDITION OF ITEM P=POOR G=GOOD F=FAIR E=EXCELLENT

BORROWER AND INFO	ITEM LOANED

NOTES	CONDITION OF ITEM
DATE OUT DATE BACK	

	P	G	F	E
OUT				
BACK				
LOAN TO AGAIN	Y		N	

BORROWER AND INFO	ITEM LOANED

NOTES	CONDITION OF ITEM
DATE OUT DATE BACK	

	P	G	F	E
OUT				
BACK				
LOAN TO AGAIN	Y		N	

KEY FOR CONDITION OF ITEM P=POOR G=GOOD F=FAIR E=EXCELLENT

BORROWER AND INFO	ITEM LOANED

NOTES	CONDITION OF ITEM
DATE OUT DATE BACK	P G F E OUT ☐☐☐☐ BACK ☐☐☐☐ LOAN TO AGAIN Y ☐ N ☐

BORROWER AND INFO	ITEM LOANED

NOTES	CONDITION OF ITEM
DATE OUT DATE BACK	P G F E OUT ☐☐☐☐ BACK ☐☐☐☐ LOAN TO AGAIN Y ☐ N ☐

KEY FOR CONDITION OF ITEM P=POOR G=GOOD F=FAIR E=EXCELLENT

BORROWER AND INFO	ITEM LOANED

NOTES	CONDITION OF ITEM
DATE OUT DATE BACK	P G F E OUT BACK LOAN TO AGAIN Y N

BORROWER AND INFO	ITEM LOANED

NOTES	CONDITION OF ITEM
DATE OUT DATE BACK	P G F E OUT BACK LOAN TO AGAIN Y N

KEY FOR CONDITION OF ITEM P=POOR G=GOOD F=FAIR E=EXCELLENT

BORROWER AND INFO	ITEM LOANED

NOTES	CONDITION OF ITEM
DATE OUT DATE BACK	P G F E OUT ☐☐☐☐ BACK ☐☐☐☐ LOAN TO AGAIN Y ☐ N ☐

BORROWER AND INFO	ITEM LOANED

NOTES	CONDITION OF ITEM
DATE OUT DATE BACK	P G F E OUT ☐☐☐☐ BACK ☐☐☐☐ LOAN TO AGAIN Y ☐ N ☐

KEY FOR CONDITION OF ITEM P=POOR G=GOOD F=FAIR E=EXCELLENT

BORROWER AND INFO	ITEM LOANED

NOTES	CONDITION OF ITEM
DATE OUT DATE BACK	P G F E OUT ☐☐☐☐ BACK ☐☐☐☐ LOAN TO AGAIN Y ☐ N ☐

BORROWER AND INFO	ITEM LOANED

NOTES	CONDITION OF ITEM
DATE OUT DATE BACK	P G F E OUT ☐☐☐☐ BACK ☐☐☐☐ LOAN TO AGAIN Y ☐ N ☐

KEY FOR CONDITION OF ITEM P=POOR G=GOOD F=FAIR E=EXCELLENT

BORROWER AND INFO	ITEM LOANED

NOTES	CONDITION OF ITEM
DATE OUT DATE BACK	P G F E OUT ☐☐☐☐ BACK ☐☐☐☐ LOAN TO AGAIN Y ☐ N ☐

BORROWER AND INFO	ITEM LOANED

NOTES	CONDITION OF ITEM
DATE OUT DATE BACK	P G F E OUT ☐☐☐☐ BACK ☐☐☐☐ LOAN TO AGAIN Y ☐ N ☐

KEY FOR CONDITION OF ITEM P=POOR G=GOOD F=FAIR E=EXCELLENT

BORROWER AND INFO

ITEM LOANED

NOTES

DATE OUT

DATE BACK

CONDITION OF ITEM

	P	G	F	E
OUT				
BACK				

LOAN TO AGAIN Y N

BORROWER AND INFO

ITEM LOANED

NOTES

DATE OUT

DATE BACK

CONDITION OF ITEM

	P	G	F	E
OUT				
BACK				

LOAN TO AGAIN Y N

KEY FOR CONDITION OF ITEM P=POOR G=GOOD F=FAIR E=EXCELLENT

BORROWER AND INFO	ITEM LOANED

NOTES	CONDITION OF ITEM
DATE OUT DATE BACK	P G F E OUT ☐☐☐☐ BACK ☐☐☐☐ LOAN TO AGAIN Y ☐ N ☐

BORROWER AND INFO	ITEM LOANED

NOTES	CONDITION OF ITEM
DATE OUT DATE BACK	P G F E OUT ☐☐☐☐ BACK ☐☐☐☐ LOAN TO AGAIN Y ☐ N ☐

KEY FOR CONDITION OF ITEM P=POOR G=GOOD F=FAIR E=EXCELLENT

Made in the USA
Monee, IL
11 November 2026

5c5b419d-59cb-4682-9b47-a1dd614ad7e3R01